S. DIONYSIVS AREOPAGITA.

THE MYSTICAL THEOLOGY
OF ST. DIONYSIUS

TRANSLATED, WITH AN
INTRODUCTION,
BY EVELYN SIRE

HOLMES PUBLISHING GROUP

ISBN 1-55818-381-7

With special thanks to Alexander McGiffert, A.B. Sharpe, and John Parkes.

Cover illustration:
An old engraving
by Michael Burghers

HOLMES PUBLISHING GROUP
POSTAL BOX 623
EDMONDS WA 98020 USA

PREFACE

The Mystic Theology is like that ladder set upon the earth whose top reached to Heaven on which the angels of God were ascending and descending, and above which stood Almighty God. The Angel ascending is the negative which distinguishes Almighty God from all created things. God is not matter — soul, mind, spirit, any being, or even being itself, but above and beyond all these. The Angel descending is the Affirmative. God is good, wise, powerful, the Being, until we come to the Symbolic Theology, which denotes Him under material forms and conditions. Theology prefers the negative because Almighty God is more appropriately presented by distinction than by comparison.

Toward the close of the fifth century there appeared a remarkable work too significant and influential to be ignored. It reveals a spirit wholly unlike that of most of the theologians of the period. Although the *Mystical Theology* was produced at a time when the Christological controversy was still absorbing attention, it shows no trace of these contemporary polemics. The author is unknown, but it is purported to be the work of Dionysius the Areopagite, referred to in the *Book of Acts* as a convert of Paul's. As such this work and others attributed to the same source were appealed to at the council of Constantinople in 533 by certain Monophysites, and though their authenticity was at first questioned, they proved immensely popular and were soon universally recognized as a genuine product of the age of the Apostles. It has long been known, however, that they could not possibly have been written at so early a day and it is now generally agreed that they originated during the fifth century. They are made up of four treatises and ten letters. The treatises, all of them addressed to Dionysius' fellow-presbyter Timothy, are entitled *The Celestial Hierarchy, The Ecclesiastical Hierarchy, Divine Names,* and *Mystical Theology,* which follows. The letters are addressed to various Christians of the first century including the apostle John. Half a dozen other works are mentioned by the writer as his own but they have altogether disappeared, if they ever existed.

The dominant theme of the extant writings is union with God. To show the importance of it and how it is to be secured was the author's chief concern. Though the writings contain considerable theology the controlling aim was not theological but religious, and the moving purpose was practical, not speculative. The author was an orthodox Trinitarian and his Christology, so far as appears from the writings we have, seems to have been sound, though somewhat monophysitic in tendency, but he was not a dogmatician and his interests lay elsewhere. The contrast between his spirit and *that* of many another theologian of the age is shown by his sixth letter addressed to the Presbyter Sosipater, in which he exhorts him not to attack those that differ with him but to set forth the truth and let it speak for itself.

The supreme good, according to Dionysius, is union with God. To be a partaker of God, to share in His divine life and thus to become deified, this is man's chief end. Salvation means deification and this involves the fullest possible likeness to God and oneness with him. The attainment of likeness to God and oneness with him *is* indeed the great aim which all should set before themselves.

The treatise on *Divine Names*, the longest of the four, is devoted to a consideration of the nature and attributes of God. At the same time though it *is* largely given up to this subject the practical aim of promoting and fostering union with God is not forgotten. In a beautiful passage in the third chapter Dionysius says that we must approach the Deity with a pure heart and with a spirit prepared for one-ness with Him. When we commune *with* Him in prayer though He seems to come to us we really go to Him. It is as if climbing up hand over hand by a chain let down from heaven we appeared to be drawing the sky downward instead of ourselves upward; or as if in a boat, pulling upon the cable that held it to the shore we appeared to be drawing the shore to the boat instead of the boat to the shore. "Wherefore," Dionysius concludes, "it is above all necessary, especially in theology, to begin with prayer, not in order to attract to ourselves the power which is present everywhere and nowhere, but by commemorating and calling upon God to give ourselves into his hands and become one with him."

There are three ways of apprehending God or three paths to a knowledge of him: the linear, as Dionysius calls it, in which we pass directly from observation of the external world to a knowledge of its cause or maker; the spiral, in which we reach God by dialectic or discursive reasoning; and the circular, in which turning away from all external things and abandoning the exercise of our reason we become mystically one with him and lose ourselves completely in him. This relationship, according to Dionysius, is the highest of all, the only complete union with God. Only in the ecstasy of mystical oneness do we really possess and enjoy him.

In the treatise on the *Divine Names*, God is represented in genuine Neo-Platonic fashion as above all being, unapproachable and incomprehensible. We are reminded of what Clement of Alexandria says of him in the eleventh chapter of the fifth book of his *Stromateis*. While the attitude reflected there was exceptional with Clement, with Dionysius it was primary and controlling. The latter could not find language strong enough to express the transcendence of God — his apartness from all that is and his complete unlikeness to it. God is beyond all being and the predicates that apply to finite things do not apply to him. In agreement with Plotinus as with Clement, Dionysius asserts that speaking literally we cannot say what God is, but only what he is not.

The most striking expression of all this is found in the last chapter of our treatise on *Mystical Theology*. After denying all corporeal and sensible qualities to the cause of all (that is, God) Dionysius continues: "We say that it is neither soul nor mind; that it is without imagination, opinion, reason, and intelligence; that it can neither be uttered nor conceived; that it is not number or order or greatness or littleness, or quality or inequality, or likeness or unlikeness; that it stands not nor moves nor rests; that it neither has power nor is power or light; that it neither lives nor is life, that it is not being nor eternity nor time; that it is not perceived by the mind; that it is neither knowledge nor truth, neither sovereignty nor wisdom, neither one nor oneness, neither divinity nor goodness; that it is not spirit as we know it, nor sonship, nor fatherhood, nor any other of the things known to us or to anyone else; that it is neither one of the things that are not nor one of the things that are; that neither do existing things know it as it is nor does it know existing things as existing; that it is devoid of reason, of name, of knowledge; that it is neither darkness nor light; neither error or truth; nor can it be in any way affirmed or denied."

God is not only above all being but above all knowledge. He is as inaccessible to the understanding *and* reason as to the bodily senses. Only the finite *can be known;* the finite is unknowable. We cannot conceive him or form an image or conception of him. We cannot name or describe him, we can only praise him. In speaking of him the language of devotion must be used rather than of ordinary discourse? Though God is incomprehensible and inaccessible to the human reason, he has revealed himself in some measure through the Scriptures and we therefore know certain things about him which would otherwise be altogether *hidden* from us. The Scriptures must be our constant guide and we must neither think nor say anything about God at variance with what is there revealed. The Scriptures do tell us of him, but these illuminations are phrased in symbolic and figurative language. We do not learn from them what God really is— that would be impossible with our finite understanding—but it is suggested to us at least in some degree what God is like, that is, not in himself but in his relations and activities. We can therefore go beyond our negations to certain positive utterances, remembering, however, that all speech about God is symbolic and can at best only point toward him, not actually describe him as he is.

Recognizing, then, the inadequacy and the figurative character of all we say we may assert that God is almighty and the source of all power and the ground of the unity of the world without whom everything would fall apart and perish. Above all being as he is, he is yet the source of all being, without whom nothing exists. All this indeed we may learn from our observation of the external world even apart from the Scriptures. God is also above all movement and life and yet without him, all life and movement are impossible. He is nameless and yet bears a great variety of names. These, however, do not characterize God in himself but only his activities and the effects he produces in us or in the world. Though God is above all knowledge he yet knows everything and is the source of all knowledge in others. At the same time this does not hinder Dionysius from asserting that the will of man is free, though he does so in a half-hearted manner.

God is also good and the source of all goodness, wise and the source of all wisdom, life and light and beauty, and the source of all these. Goodness and beauty are one in God and from him come all the goodness and beauty in the universe. As the sun warms the earth without trying to do so, simply because of what it is, so the goodness of God is without effort on his part and men are blessed by it, because God is what he is. Dionysius has much to say about the love of God. God is love and all love is of God. It is from him, through him and to him. Love unites and by it all separations and divisions are overcome. Because of this Divine love, the unities in the world are mightier than the divisions.

Yet if God is good, how is the existence of evil to be explained? Faced with this question Dionysius answers in good Neo-Platonic fashion that evil is nothing positive; it is only a defect, the absence of good. Being is good, only the lack of it is evil. Evil does not reside in matter; in fact, it has no real existence anywhere and no efficient cause. It is due to weakness not power, to the want of being and of the good not to the presence of anything positive. Nothing is mightier than the real unless it partakes of good. In so far as good is lacking, then reality is lacking. All things strive toward good, even the demons, which means that *all* strive toward being and reality. Evil is only for the sake of good and is overruled by providence for good ends. Although there is considerable theology and no *little* philosophy in this little treatise, its motive is not theological *per se* or even philosophical but religious and practical and which we will explore briefly.

In the *Mystical Theology*, Dionysius reaches the summit of his thought in a genuine and thoroughgoing mysticism. He sets forth in emphatic language, language that has become classic in the literature of mysticism, what he regards as the highest kind of union with God. Addressing his fellow-presbyter Timothy he exhorts him to free himself from all entanglements, and following the *via negativa* which means the repudiation of all the affirmations of the reason and the abandonment of all definite ideas, to lose himself in God in the ecstasy of mystical oneness with him. For ordinary Christians the author evidently thinks that oneness with God attained through the sacraments and other symbolic ceremonies is enough and that no more can be expected of them. However, for Timothy and others like him, a higher blessedness is possible, to be attained not by the use of sacred rites or by the assistance of sacred persons (neither the sacraments nor the clergy are mentioned in this treatise), but by the way of genuine mysticism. "Do thou, dear Timothy, in thy eager striving after mystical visions abandon both sense-perception and mental activity, all things sensible and intellectual, all being and not being, and as far as is possible mount up without knowledge into union with the One who is above all being and knowledge; for by freeing thyself completely and unconditionally from thyself and from all things, thou shalt come to the super-essential brightness of the divine darkness, if thou turnest thy back on everything and art loosed from everything. But take care that this come not to the ears of the uninitiated, who being entangled in existing things imagine that there is nothing super-essential above the things that are and suppose that they can grasp with their understanding the One who has made the darkness his hiding place." With this may be compared the following passage from one of Dionysius' epistles: "If anyone seeing God understands what he has seen, he has not seen him but some one of his creatures that are and are known. But God himself, raised above mind and being, in that he is wholly unknown and is not, both exists in a super-essential manner and is known in a super-mental way."

The extreme mysticism of the tract on *Mystical Theology*, of which preparation was given already in the treatise on *Divine Names*, was not wholly new in the Eastern church. Traces of similar doctrines and philosophical ideas are found in Clement of Alexandria, Gregory of Nyssa, Athanasius the Great and other early Christian writers, but by none of them was it carried as far as by Dionysius who in this matter was completely at one with the great Neo-Platonist, Plotinus. If we would reach God, Plotinus insisted as Dionysius *did* after him, we must rise above knowledge into ecstasy. In this ecstatic state, though we do not understand God, we may be said most truly to enjoy him. It is worth noticing in this connection that like Plotinus, Dionysius seems to have thought of mystical and ecstatic union with God as a rare thing, open only to certain choice spirits and to

11

them only occasionally and as the result of severe discipline or sublime Grace.

It is commonly taken for granted *that* our author was a Neoplatonist before he became a Christian and brought his Neoplatonism over into the church with him. Whether this be true or not, he did reflect its influence at several points, particularly as represented by his older contemporary Proclus. Not only his mysticism, with its three stages of approach to the Divine, but also his idea of God, his theory of the nature of evil, and his symbolism, in principle if not in form, all had their antecedents in that system and were unquestionably derived in part at least if not wholly therefrom.

The influence of the Pseudo-Dionysian writings was enormous. It was due to them in no small part that the Eastern church of the Middle Ages was a genuine mystery-cult not only in fact but in theory as well. In them were set out more clearly than in any other Christian documents of the ancient church the principles that constitute a true Mystery Religion:—a sacred ritual with secret and symbolic rites which are open only to the initiated, and through which a knowledge of divine things is imparted and a man enters into union with the divine, is made a partaker of immortality, and becomes progressively deified. This was not new in the Eastern church. From the earliest days, Christianity in its Pauline form bore the aspect of a Mystery Religion and owed its spread in no small part to that fact. But Dionysius carried the matter further than anyone before him and gave classic expression to this interpretation of the Christian religion.

And still more, thoroughgoing mysticism of the Neo-platonic type was widely fostered and was given an increasing currency by the reading of his works. Their credit and authority were the greater because it was believed that their author belonged to the apostolic age. They were brief writings and contained only a few closely related and exceedingly seductive ideas. These were iterated and reiterated with the utmost persistence and had much to do with their vogue. Nor was their reputation confined to the east. Before the end of the sixth century they were referred to by Gregory the Great and in the ninth century they were translated into Latin by Scotus Erigena. Much use was made of them by several of the schoolmen. Hugo of St. Victor wrote a commentary on them and Thomas Aquinas esteemed them highly. Dante appears to have been indebted to them as well. Their influence was especially great in the realm of mysticism. Indeed, it would hardly be too much to say that they were the fountain head of most of the mysticism in the Latin church of the Middle Ages.

I

Of the Divine and Holy Darkness

Exalted Trinity! Hear me. You are the transcendence of all knowledge and principle with a goodness surpassing understanding. Guide all Christians with holy affirmation if Divine wisdom stands closest to their hearts. Bring us to the Real through your Oracles and submit us to an understanding exceeding incomprehensibility, eclipsing luminosity, and surpassing exaltation. Only through these excesses, most lucid and glorified One, can we know the Mysteries of the truth within the great and hidden Light—a Light of awful Silence residing in a Darkness surpassing sense. Of the above, I say: This is my prayer!

For you, dear Timothy, here is the way of mystical contemplation. Leave behind the intellect and sensation of existence, cease not in the renunciation of yourself, and seek to *unknow* the operations of the intellect regarding the things that are and the things that are not. Do this so you may be taken above knowledge into the Divine Darkness beyond existence.

Disclose this wisdom to none but initiates of our Faith, for those who cling to the objects of human invention cannot receive this. For they imagine that there is nought beyond their own limits and claim the non-existence of a reality beyond their conceptions. If captive of this construct, one can never know

Him who makes Darkness his secret hiding place. If the essence of the Mysteries is above the understanding of ones such as these, what could be said of those even more ignorant who call the Lord of the First Cause after the lowest things in nature and fashion their non-gods and false beings in error? If they were in Wisdom, they would declare Him as Cause of all — this Cause being all that may be described positively regarding Him, for where God is concerned, denial is not contrary to affirmation, since He is infinitely above all notion of deprivation, and above all affirmation and negation as well.

The divine Bartholomew says that Theology is both much and minute, and that the Gospel is like unto it for it also is great and ample, and yet short. I believe his meaning to be sublime for the beneficent cause of all things says much, and says little, and is altogether silent. This signifies that the goodly Cause of all is most eloquent, yet the Cause utters few words or is completely silent where man is concerned, for He has neither (human) speech nor (human) understanding, because He is super-essentially exalted above created things. His unveiling is through His naked Truth and is for those alone who pass beyond all that is either pure or impure. You must ascend above the heights of holy things, abandon light and sound and even heavenly or spiritual perception, that you may be absorbed into the holy Darkness where, as the scripture says, He truly is.

There was a deep meaning in God's command that the good Moses should first purify himself, and then to separate himself from the impure. After his purification, he heard the voices of many trumpets and saw many lights with beams of purity. After this, he was thereafter separated from the multitude and together with the elect priests, he came to the summit of the divine ascent. Evenso, he did not attain the presence of God as He is (for He cannot be looked upon), but Moses was cognizant of the place where the Divine was though this be beyond the possibilities and conceptions of even the holy imagination of God's servant. In this holy Place, the seeker, who is free and untrammeled by all that can be seen and all that sees, can enter into the true mystical darkness of ignorance, whence all perception of understanding is excluded. Here the seeker may abide in that which is intangible and invisible, being wholly absorbed in Him who is beyond all things, and belong no more to any, neither to himself or to another, but is united in his higher self to Him who can only be understood after a manner above the mind.

II

How we ought to be united with and render
praise to the Cause of all and above all

We desire that we may abide in this Darkness which is beyond light. Without seeing and without knowing, we hope to see and to know that which is above sight and knowledge through the realization that we see not and we know not. For this knowledge is to truly understand and know the Divine and thus praise, superessentially, Him Who is superessential, by the abstraction of the essence of all things. Even as those who would form a statue out of marble must abstract or remove all the surrounding material which hinders the vision which the marble conceals, and thus, bring to light the hidden beauty.

It is needful to make this abstraction in a manner precisely opposite from the way we deal with the Divine attributes. In other words, to distinguish this negative method of abstraction from the positive method of affirmation. For with these latter we begin with the universal and primary, and pass through the intermediate and secondary to the particular and ultimate attributes; but now we ascend from the particular to the universal conceptions, abstracting all attributes in order that, without veil, we may know that Unknowing, which is enshrouded under all that is known and all that can be known, and that we may begin to contemplate the superessential Darkness which is hidden by all the light that is in existing things.

III

Of the affirmative and negative expressions of God

In *Theological Outlines*, we celebrated the principal affirmative expressions respecting God —

How the Divine and good Nature is spoken of as One and is also Three.

What is that within it which is spoken of as Paternity and Sonship.

What the Divine name of "the Holy Spirit" is meant to signify.

How from the immaterial and indivisible Good the perfect Lights dwelling in the heart of Goodness sprang forth and remained, yet remained one with the Divine Nature and with all else besides.

How the superessential Jesus became the substance of veritable human nature.

How we made known heavenly things from the Scriptures in the *Theological Outlines*.

And in the treatise concerning *Divine Names*, how He is named all Good and all Being and all Life and all Wisdom and all Power—and whatever else belongs to the nomenclature of God.

Further, in the *Symbolical Theology*, we pointed to questions immense as in:

What are the Names transferred from objects of sense to things Divine?

What are the Divine forms and what the Divine appearances and parts?

What are the Divine places and ornaments?

What are the angers and the griefs and the Divine wrath?

What are the carousals, and the ensuing sicknesses?

What are the oaths and the curses?

What are the sleepings, and what the awakenings?

— and all the other Divinely formed representations, which belong to the description of God, through symbols. I imagine that you have seen how the lowest are expressed in somewhat more words than the first. For, it was necessary that the *Theological Outlines*, and the unfolding of the *Divine Names* should be expressed in fewer words than the *Symbolic Theology*; since, in proportion as we ascend to the higher, in such a degree the expressions are circumscribed by the contemplations of the things intelligible. As even now, when entering into the gloom which is above mind, we shall find, not little speaking, but a complete absence of speech, and absence of conception. In the other case, the discourse, in descending from the above to the lowest, is widened according to the descent, to a proportionate extent; but now, in ascending from below to that which is above, in proportion to the ascent, it is contracted, and after a complete ascent, it will become wholly voiceless, and will be wholly united to the unutterable. But, for what reason in short, you say, having attributed the Divine attributes from the foremost, do we begin the Divine abstraction from things lowest? Because it is necessary that they who place attributes on that which is above every attribute, should place the attributive affirmation from that which is more cognate to it; but that they who abstract, with regard to that which is above every abstraction, should make the abstraction from things which are further removed from it. Are not life and goodness more (cognate) than air and stone? and He is not given to debauch and to wrath, more (removed) than He is not expressed nor conceived.

IV

*That He who is the supreme cause of all sensible things
is Himself no part of those things*

We say then that the Cause of all, which is above all, is neither without being nor without life. It is not without reason and not without mind, nor is He a body, for He is neither form or shape, quality or quantity. He is not placed or visible or tangible. He is neither sensitive or perceives by the senses. He is subject to no disorder or disturbance arising from the earthy passions of matter. He is never powerless and never subject to random hazard. He does not require light. He is beyond change, decay, corruption, division, deprivation, and flux. He is not subject to anything that belongs to the senses.

V

*That He who is the supreme cause of all intelligible
things is Himself no part of those things*

On the other hand, ascending, we say, that He who is God is not:—

SOUL
INTELLECT
IMAGINATION
OPINION
REASON
CONCEPTION
SPEECH
UNDERSTANDING

For He who is God cannot be —:

EXPRESSED
CONCEIVED
NUMBERED
ORDERED
QUANTIFIED
QUALIFIED
THINGS THAT ARE
THINGS THAT ARE NOT

He is not equality or inequality. He is not similarity or dissimilarity. He does not stand or move or rest. He has not power or is power. He is not light or dark. He neither lives or is life. He is not age or time or essence. He is not truth or knowledge and is not subject to a touch intelligible. He is neither one or unity or divinity or goodness. He is not even Spirit (as we know spirit). He is not Fatherhood or the Son–Spirit of Eternity or any other thing whatsoever known to us, or known to any other existing being. He is not expression, name or knowledge. He is neither light or darkness. He is neither truth or error. Neither is there any definition at all of It, nor any abstraction. But when making the predications and abstractions of things after It, we neither predicate, nor abstract from It, since the all-perfect and sole Cause of all is above all affirmation, and that which transcends all is above all subtraction, being He Who is absolutely freed from everything and absolutely separate and beyond all that is or will be.

For a Complete List of Publications,
Please address:
HOLMES PUBLISHING GROUP
POSTAL BOX 623
EDMONDS WA 98020 USA